Independent Schools
Examinations Board

MATHEMATICS POCKET NOTES

David E Hanson

www.galorepark.co.uk

Independent Schools
Examinations Board

GALORE PARK

Published by ISEB Publications, an imprint of Galore Park
Publishing Ltd, 19/21 Sayers Lane, Tenterden, Kent TN30 6BW

www.galorepark.co.uk

Text copyright © David E Hanson 2004

The right of David E Hanson to be identified as the author of
this Work has been asserted by him in accordance with sections
77 and 78 of the Copyright, Designs and Patents Act 1988.

Printed and bound in the UK by Charlesworth Press, Wakefield

ISBN: 978 0903627 14 6

All rights reserved: no part of this publication may be sold,
reproduced, stored in a retrieval system, or transmitted in any
form or by any means, electronic, mechanical, photocopying,
recording or otherwise, without the prior permission of the
copyright owner or a licence permitting restricted copying issued
by the Copyright Licensing Agency, 90 Tottenham Court Road,
London W1P 0LP.

Published 2004, reprinted 2007, 2009, 2010, 2012

Details of other ISEB revision guides, publications and
examination papers are available at www.galorepark.co.uk

Front cover image: Steven May/Alamy

CONTENTS

1. NUMBERS 1
   1.1 Properties of numbers 1
   1.2 Place value; ordering 1
   1.3 Estimation and approximation 2
   1.4 Fractions, decimals, percentages; ratio 2

2. CALCULATIONS 4
   2.1 Number operations 4
   2.2 Mental strategies 4
   2.3 Written methods 5
   2.4 Calculator methods 5
   2.5 Checking results 6

3. PROBLEM SOLVING 7
   3.1 Decision making 7
   3.2 Reasoning about numbers or shapes 7
   3.3 Real-life mathematics 7

4. ALGEBRA 8
   4.1 Equations and formulae 8
   4.2 Sequences and functions 10
   4.3 Graphs 10

5. SHAPE, SPACE AND MEASURES 12
   5.1 Measures 12
   5.2 Shape 13
   5.3 Space 14

6. HANDLING DATA 18
   6.1 Data Handling 18
   6.2 Probability 22

7. COMMON AREAS OF CONFUSION 23

NOTE FROM AUTHOR

I hope that these notes may prove useful for those who readily forget, and serve as reminders in the final stages of preparation for examinations.

ACKNOWLEDGEMENT

I am grateful to Oliver Smyth, of Brighton College, leader of the ISEB 13+ Mathematics setting team, for his helpful suggestions and encouragement.

1. NUMBERS

1.1 PROPERTIES OF NUMBERS

- An **integer** is a whole number (positive, negative or zero).
- 42 is the **product** of 6 and 7
- 12 and 18 are **multiples** of 6
- 1, 2, 3, 4, 6 and 12 are the **factors** of 12
- 64 is the **square** of 8 (written 8^2)
- 7 is the **square root** of 49 (written $\sqrt{49}$)
- 8 is the **cube** of 2 (written 2^3)
- 4 is the **cube root** of 64 (written $\sqrt[3]{64}$)
- 2, 3, 5, 7, 11, 13, 17, 19, 23, 29 are the first ten **primes**.
- 72 written as a **product of primes**, using **index notation**, is $2^3 \times 3^2$

- $6 \times 7 = 42$ $6 \times 8 = 48$ $6 \times 9 = 54$
  $7 \times 7 = 49$ $7 \times 8 = 56$ $7 \times 9 = 63$
  $8 \times 8 = 64$ $8 \times 9 = 72$ $9 \times 9 = 81$

- $^-2 + 3 = 1$ $^-2 - 3 = {^-5}$ $^-2 \times 3 = {^-6}$
  $^-2 + {^-3} = {^-5}$ $^-2 - {^-3} = 1$ $^-2 \times {^-3} = 6$

- $^-6 \div 2 = {^-3}$ $^-6 \div {^-2} = 3$ $6 \div {^-2} = {^-3}$

1.2 PLACE VALUE; ORDERING

- Multiplying by 10, move digits one place left in relation to the decimal point:
      TU.t   HTU
      $32.5 \times 10 = 325$

  Dividing by 100, move digits two places right in relation to the decimal point:
      U.th   U.th
      $4.75 \div 100 = 0.0475$

- 0.213   0.312   1.32   2.13   2.31   3.12   3.21 are in order of increasing size

- • $x < 3$ means x is less than 3
  • $x \geq {^-2}$ means x is greater than or equal to $^-2$

1.3 ESTIMATION AND APPROXIMATION

- 37 **rounded** to the nearest ten is 40
  205 rounded to the nearest ten is 210
  140 rounded to the nearest hundred is 100
- 3.449 written to one **decimal place** (d.p.) is 3.4
  3.449 written to two decimal places is 3.45
- 0.6050 is written to 4 **significant figures** (s.f.)
- When **estimating** the result of a calculation, first write each number correct to 1 significant figure:

  $\dfrac{3.81 \times 9.15}{1.73 + 1.06}$ becomes $\dfrac{4 \times 9}{2 + 1}$

  calculate using the rounded figures $\dfrac{36}{3} = 12$

- An **approximate** value of $\dfrac{3.81 \times 9.15}{1.73 + 1.06}$ is 12

1.4 FRACTIONS, DECIMALS, PERCENTAGES; RATIO

- A **fraction** compares part of a whole to the whole:

  $\dfrac{3}{5}$ means 3 parts of a whole containing 5 parts

- A fraction can be written as a **decimal** by:
  - first writing an **equivalent fraction** with a denominator of 10, 100, 1000 etc. if possible:

  $\dfrac{3}{5}$ becomes $\dfrac{6}{10}$ which can be written 0.6

  - dividing the **numerator** (top number) by the **denominator** (bottom number).
- A **percentage** is a number of parts out of 100:

  $\dfrac{3}{4}$ becomes $\dfrac{75}{100}$ which can be written 75%

- 75% of £80 is £80 $\times \dfrac{75}{100}$ which gives £60

- A **ratio** can compare two or more parts:
  for a class of 7 boys and 8 girls, we can write
  - ratio number of boys to girls is 7 : 8
  - ratio number of girls to the class is 8 : 15
- Fractions and ratios can be written in their **simplest form** (**lowest terms**):
  - $\frac{20}{30}$ in its simplest form is $\frac{2}{3}$
  - the ratio 36 : 45 simplifies to 4 : 5
- When adding or subtracting fractions, change one or both to equivalent fractions with same denominator:

  $\frac{3}{5} + \frac{1}{2} = \frac{6}{10} + \frac{5}{10}$ which gives $\frac{11}{10}$

  $\frac{11}{10}$ is an **improper** (top heavy) fraction

  $\frac{11}{10} = 1\frac{1}{10}$ a **mixed number**
- When multiplying or dividing fractions, change mixed numbers to **improper** fractions first.
  - $\frac{3}{5} \times 1\frac{1}{2}$ becomes $\frac{3}{5} \times \frac{3}{2}$ which gives $\frac{9}{10}$
  - $\frac{3}{5} \div \frac{1}{2}$ becomes $\frac{3}{5} \times \frac{2}{1}$ which gives $\frac{6}{5}$

    which can be changed to $1\frac{1}{5}$
- A **proportion** is part of a whole and can be expressed as a fraction, decimal or percentage.
  - things are in **proportion** if they maintain a stated relationship, as in the example: $\frac{1}{2}$ cup of porridge oats is mixed with $1\frac{1}{4}$ cups of milk to make porridge for one person, 2 cups of porridge oats are mixed with 5 cups of milk to make porridge for four people.

2. CALCULATIONS

2.1 NUMBER OPERATIONS

- When a **division** is not exact, it may be appropriate to:
  - write a **remainder**: 5 ÷ 3 = 1 remainder 2
  - continue (with decimals if necessary) until an exact answer is reached: 3 ÷ 8 = 0.375
  - write a **recurring decimal**: 5 ÷ 3 = 1.66666... which we can shorten to 1.6̇ (note the dot over the 6)
  - write the answer to a number of decimal places.
- When multiplying a given number by a number between 0 and 1 the result is smaller: 7 × 0.6 = 4.2
- When dividing a given number by a number between 0 and 1 the result is bigger: 16 ÷ 0.5 = 32
- The **order of operations** is very important:
  Brackets
  Index numbers (or powers)
  Divide
  Multiply (including 'of')
  Add
  Subtract

2.2 MENTAL STRATEGIES

- Make use of factors:
  72 ÷ 18 becomes 72 ÷ 2 and then 36 ÷ 9
- Make use of known facts:
  6 × 2 = 12 so 0.6 × 200 = 120
- Make use of step by step approach:

  $\frac{5}{8}$ of 40 (find $\frac{1}{8}$ and then multiply by 5)

  15% of 45 (find 10%, then 5%, then add)

  $17\frac{1}{2}$% of £12 (find 10%, then 5%, then $2\frac{1}{2}$%, then add)

2.3 WRITTEN METHODS

- Watch place value: TU.th
                                          3.95
                                        +10.7

- A carefully set out calculation can help you to avoid errors and gain more marks.

EXAMPLES

Addition

$3.95 + 10.7$

```
   3.95
+ 10.7
  14.65
```

Subtraction

$7.1 - 4.68$

```
   7.10
-  4.68
   2.42
```

Multiplication

126×64

```
    126        126        126
  ×  64      ×  64      ×  64
    504        504        504
    1 2        7560       7560
               1 3        8064
```

Division

$384 \div 5$

```
        076.8
       ┌──────
    5 │ 384.0
        3 3 4
```

2.4 CALCULATOR METHODS

- Calculators vary; they may:
  - have different key labels
  - do calculations in different ways.

- You should be familiar with:
  - negative numbers **+/−** or **(−)**
  - memory **Min MR** or alternatives
  - brackets **(.. ..)**
  - fractions $a\frac{b}{c}$
  - **%** for percentages
  - squares x^2
  - square roots √
  - indices x^n
  - cube roots $^3\sqrt{}$
  - π for calculations involving circles.
- Interpreting the display:
  - | − 2. | negative 2
  - | 29.5 | £29.50 (money)
    29 min 30 sec (time)
    $29\frac{1}{2}$
  - | 1⌐3⌐4 | $1\frac{3}{4}$ (fractions)
  - | 1.9999999 | 2 (truncated recurring decimal)
  - | 2.5 − 03 | 2.5×10^{-3} (0.0025)
    standard index form
    | 2.5⁻⁰³ | (scientific notation)

2.5 CHECKING RESULTS

- Do the reverse calculation:

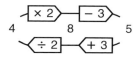

- Do an alternative calculation.
- Estimate, using approximations.

3. PROBLEM SOLVING

3.1 DECISION MAKING

- Choose a suitable strategy:
    - make an organised list (all possible outcomes)
    - try a practical approach (draw diagrams etc.)
    - guess and check (trial and improvement)
    - try a simpler example (try easier numbers etc.)
    - look for a pattern (and extend to next one)
    - generalise and test (form a 'rule' or **formula** and test it before using it).

3.2 REASONING ABOUT NUMBERS OR SHAPES

- Make use of knowledge and observations.
- Ask 'What if . . .?'
- Helpful hints:
    - read instructions carefully to make sure that you know what is required; look out for the important word 'not'
    - draw a sketch if that is appropriate
    - make an outline plan of your strategy
    - write down clearly what you are doing so that someone else can follow easily

3.3 REAL LIFE MATHEMATICS

- Work often involves:
    - shopping
    - currency conversions
    - fractions and percentages
    - ratio and proportion.

4. ALGEBRA

4.1 EQUATIONS AND FORMULAE

- x a number we don't know.
- $2x$ twice x $\qquad$ $\frac{1}{3}x$ or $\frac{x}{3}$ a third of x
- $x + 2$ two more than x
- x^2 x squared $x \times x$ • x^3 x cubed $x \times x \times x$
- $4x^2$ 4 times x^2
- $2x^3 - 3$ three less than twice x^3
- x^2 is a **term**.
- $x - 3$ is an **expression** in terms of x with 2 terms.
- $x^2 + 2x + 3$ has three terms.
- x, $3x$ and ^-2x are **like** terms; x^2, $4x^2$ and $^-5x^2$ are **like** terms.
- Expressions can be simplified by **collecting like terms**:
  $8x^2 + 3x - x^2 - 3 \to 7x^2 + 3x - 3$
- Expressions can be **factorised** by putting in **brackets**:
  $x^2 - 4x \to x(x - 4)$
- Brackets can be **multiplied out**:
  $$3(2x + 4) \to 6x + 12$$
- We can find the value of an expression by **substitution** if we are told the value of the unknown number(s): $x = 5$; $y = ^-2$
  $$4x - 3y \to 4 \times 5 - 3 \times ^-2 \to 26$$
- $3x - 5 = 10$ is an **equation**.
- We can **solve** an equation to find the value of the unknown number:
  - $2x = 6$ • $x + 4 = 12$ • $\frac{x}{2} = 9$
  - $\to x = 3$ $\qquad \to x = 8 \qquad \to x = 18$
- $4x + 2 < 14$ is an **inequality**.
- We can solve an inequality to discover something about the unknown number.
  - $4x \leq 8$ • $x + 3 > 1$
  - $\to x \leq 2$ $\qquad \to x > ^-2$

  The integer values satisfying both are $^-1, 0, 1, 2$

- When solving complicated equations or inequalities do one step at a time.
- A **formula** is a set of instructions for calculating an unknown quantity; it will have one dependent **variable** (the one standing for the result); it will have one or more independent variables.
  - $A = \frac{1}{2}bh$ formula for the area of a triangle
    A is dependent; b and h are independent
  - a formula becomes an equation when numbers are substituted
  - if we know the values of all but one of the variables, we can find the value of the other.
- We can solve a **quadratic equation** by **trial and improvement**.
  For the quadratic equation $x^2 + 5x - 25 = 0$ we could guess that x is 3
  We get $9 + 15 - 25 = {}^-1$, so 3 is a little too small.
  We improve our guess.
  Clearly 4 would be much too big, so we could try 3.2 for the value of x.
  We get $10.24 + 16 - 25 = 1.24$ which is too large.
  A next sensible guess for the value of x would be 3.1
  Quadratic equations can have two different roots.

4.2 SEQUENCES AND FUNCTIONS

- 1, 4, 7, 10, ... is a **sequence**.
  - there is an 'add 3' rule to get the next term
  - the nth term is given by the expression $3n - 2$
- $y = x + 3$ is a **linear function**.
  - a table of **input** (x) and **output** (y) values can be prepared

x	-1	0	1	2	3	4
y	2	3	4	5	6	7

- $y = x^2 - 4$ is a **quadratic function**.

  -

x	-2	-1	0	1	2	3
y	0	-3	-4	-3	0	5

4.3 GRAPHS

- A function can be represented on a **co-ordinate** grid by plotting **ordered pairs** of (input, output) values and drawing a **line** or **curve** through them.
  - $y = x + 3$ $(-1,2)$, $(0,3)$, $(1,4)$, $(2,5)$ etc.
  - $y = x^2 - 4$ $(-2,0)$, $(-1,-3)$, $(0,-4)$, $(1,-3)$ etc.

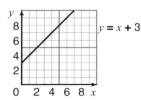
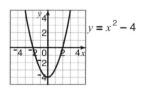

  - the line or curve is the **graph** of the function.

- **Simultaneous equations** $\quad y - x = 5$
  $\qquad\qquad\qquad\qquad\qquad\; y + 2x = 17$

This can be solved:
- graphically by drawing both lines to find the co-ordinates of **intersection** (4,9)

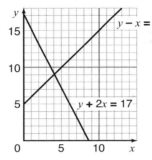

- by **substitution**   • by **elimination**.

5. SHAPE, SPACE AND MEASURES

5.1 MEASURES

- **Metric units**
  - length: 1 **km** = 1000 **m**; 1 **m** = 100 **cm**; 1 **cm** = 10 **mm**
  - area: 1 **km**^{2} = 100 **ha**; 1 **ha** = 10000 **m**^{2}; 1 **m**^{2} = 10000 **cm**^{2}
  - mass: 1 **tonne** = 1000 **kg**; 1 **kg** = 1000 **g**; 1 **g** = 1000 **mg**
  - capacity: 1 **litre** = 100 **cl**; 1 **cl** = 10 **ml**.
- **Imperial units**
  - length: 1 **mile** = 1760 **yards**; 1 **yard** = 3 **feet**; 1 **foot** = 12 **inches**
  - capacity: 1 **gallon** = 8 **pints**.
- Metric/imperial equivalents:
  - 1 kg is about 2.2 lb
  - 30 g is about 1 ounce
  - 8 km is about 5 miles
  - 90 cm is about 1 yard
  - 2.5 cm is about 1 inch
  - 4.5 litres is about 1 gallon
  - 1 litre is just less than 2 pints.
- Perimeter formulae:
  - rectangle $\quad p = 2(l + w)$
  - circle circumference $\quad c = 2\pi r$
- Area formulae:
  - triangle $\quad A = \frac{1}{2}bh$
  - trapezium $\quad A = \frac{1}{2}(a + b)h$
  - circle $\quad A = \pi r^2$
- Volume formulae:
  - cuboid $\quad V = lwh$
  - cylinder $\quad V = \pi r^2 h$
- **Speed** is the distance travelled in 1 unit of time:
  - metres per second (**m/s**)
  - kilometres per hour (**km/h**)
  - miles per hour (**mph** or **miles/h**).

5.2 SHAPE

- **Quadrilaterals**
  - equal sides and angles are indicated
  - number of lines of symmetry (**L**) is given
  - order of rotational symmetry (**O**) is given
    (order 1 means **no** rotational symmetry).

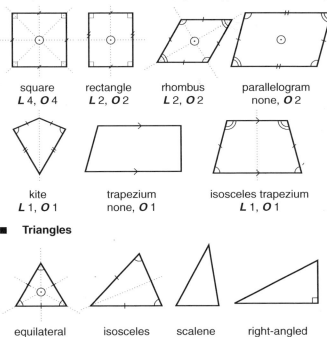

square
L 4, **O** 4

rectangle
L 2, **O** 2

rhombus
L 2, **O** 2

parallelogram
none, **O** 2

kite
L 1, **O** 1

trapezium
none, **O** 1

isosceles trapezium
L 1, **O** 1

- **Triangles**

equilateral
L 3, **O** 3

isosceles
L 1, **O** 1

scalene
none, **O** 1

right-angled
none, **O** 1
(unless isosceles)

- Other **plane** (2-dimensional) shapes (**polygons**)
  - 5 sides: pentagon, 6: hexagon, 7: heptagon, 8: octagon, 9: nonagon, 10: decagon
  - n-sided **regular** polygons have all sides and angles equal; they have n lines of symmetry and rotational symmetry of order n.
- **Solid** (3-dimensional) **shapes**

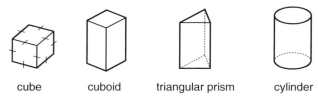

cube   cuboid   triangular prism   cylinder

5.3 SPACE

- **Lines**

- **perpendicular**   • **parallel**

- **Points of the compass**

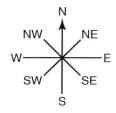

- **3 figure bearings**
  - always **clockwise** from the direction of **north** from 000° to 360°
  - always three figures.

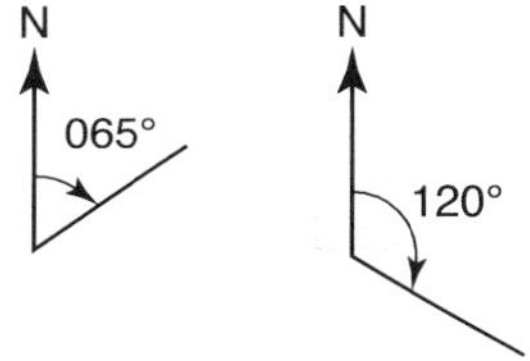

- **Angles**

acute <90°   right 90°   obtuse 90°< <180°   straight 180°   reflex >180°

- Angles which are equal

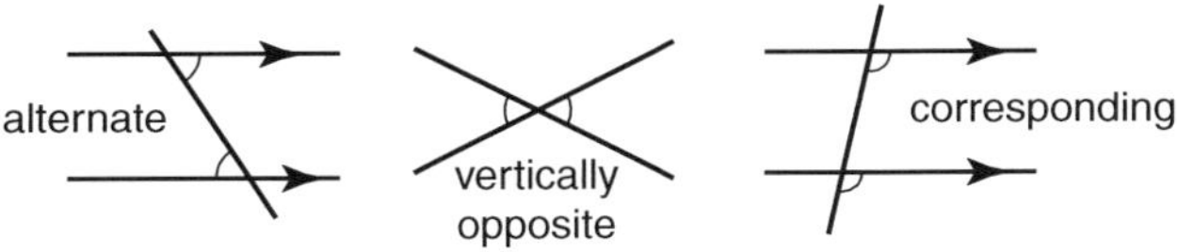

  alternate   vertically opposite   corresponding

- Angles which add up to 180°

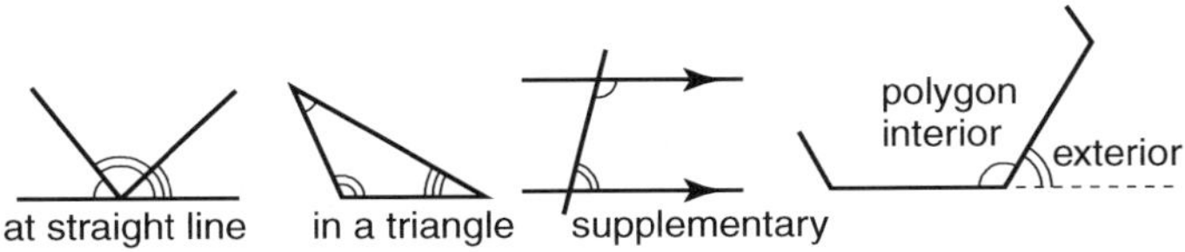

  at straight line   in a triangle   supplementary   polygon interior / exterior

- Angles which add up to 360°

  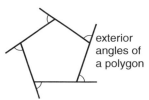

at a point   in a quadrilateral   exterior angles of a polygon

- Other angle sums

 regular pentagon interior angle sum
$5 \times 108° \rightarrow 540°$

 $3 \times 180° \rightarrow 540°$

- **Transformations**
  - **reflection** in a line

  - **rotation** about a point, through an angle, **anticlockwise** unless stated otherwise

180°

90° clockwise (or ⁻90°)

- **translation** on a co-ordinate grid
  example: 9 units right; 4 units up

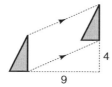

- **enlargement** by a **scale factor**.

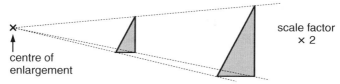

if the length scale factor is 3 then the area scale factor is 9

- **Scale drawings** often involve the use of
  - 3 figure bearings
  - ruler and set square to draw parallel north lines
  - compasses to draw arcs
- **Pythagoras' theorem** for a right-angled triangle:

  $h^2 = a^2 + b^2$ where h is the **hypotenuse**.

- **Trigonometry** (not in CE)

  $\sin x = \dfrac{p}{h}$, $\cos x = \dfrac{q}{h}$, $\tan x = \dfrac{p}{q}$

  $\sin y = \dfrac{q}{h}$, $\cos y = \dfrac{p}{h}$, $\tan y = \dfrac{q}{p}$

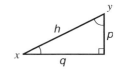

6. HANDLING DATA

6.1 DATA HANDLING

- **Raw data** can be collected (recorded) in:
  - a list
  - a table
  - a tally.

head/tail
tails
heads
heads
tails
heads
tails
heads
heads

name	glasses	blond/e
Ann	✓	✓
Bill		✓
Clare	✓	✓
Dan	✓	
Ellie		
Fred	✓	
Gill	✓	✓
Hal		✓

score on die		
score	tally	frequency
1	IIII III	8
2	IIII IIII III	13
3	IIII IIII I	11
4	IIII III	8
5	IIII IIII I	11
6	IIII IIII	9
total		60

Raw data can sometimes be **sorted** (**grouped**) using a **flowchart**.

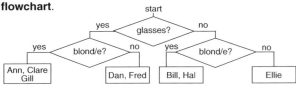

- Collected raw data can sometimes be **collated** into a **frequency table**, using suitable **class intervals** if appropriate.
- Data can be represented, where appropriate, in a:
  - **Venn diagram**
  - **Carroll diagram**

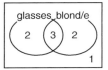

not blond/e	2	1
blond/e	3	2

glasses   no glasses

- **pictogram**
  one symbol represents
  one toss

- **block graph**
  one block represents
  one toss

heads   tails

In pictograms and block graphs one symbol or one block can sometimes represent two or more, and fractions of a symbol or block may appear.

- **bar chart**
- **bar line graph**

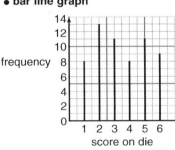

- **frequency diagram**

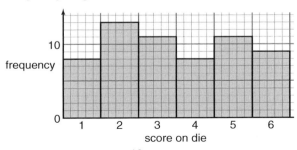

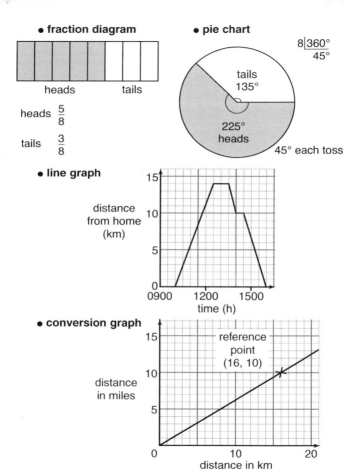

- **scatter diagram (graph)**

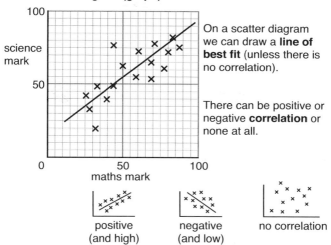

On a scatter diagram we can draw a **line of best fit** (unless there is no correlation).

There can be positive or negative **correlation** or none at all.

positive (and high)   negative (and low)   no correlation

- The **range** of a set of raw data is the difference between the largest and smallest values.
  - the range of these scores out of ten is 4 (9−5)

  5 6 7 7 8 8 8 9

- The **mean** of the set of scores is found by adding the scores and dividing by the number of scores
  58 ÷ 8 which gives 7.25
- The **median** of the set of scores is the middle one when they are arranged in order (or in this case the mean of the middle two) which is 7.5
- The **mode** is the most common score, 8
- When people talk simply about *the average*, they usually refer to the mean but the mode or median may sometimes be more useful:
  shoe sizes (mode); exam marks (median).

6.2 PROBABILITY

- **Probability** is a number which measures the likelihood of an event happening.
- The likelihood can be described as: impossible, unlikely, even chance, likely, certain.
- A **probability scale** runs from 0 (no chance/impossible) to 1 (certain).

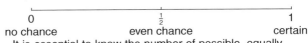

- It is essential to know the number of possible, equally likely, **outcomes** to an event and it is worth listing them.

regular pentagonal spinner
5 equally likely outcomes

fair ordinary die

6 equally likely outcomes

- The **probability** of an event happening is usually expressed as a fraction (sometimes as %):

$$\frac{3}{5} \qquad \frac{\text{number of successes}}{\text{number of outcomes}}$$

- The **experimental** probability may not be the same as the **expected** (calculated) probability:
  - the number of trials may be too small
  - the die or spinner may be **biased** (unfair).
- The sum of the probabilities of all possible outcomes of an event is 1
- Outcomes of two events at the same time:
  - two coins: HH, HT, TH, TT (4 outcomes)
    probability of two heads $\frac{1}{4}$
    probability of one head and one tail $\frac{1}{2}$
  - two ordinary dice: 36 outcomes.

7. COMMON AREAS OF CONFUSION

- **Letters**
  - **CAPITALS**
    - labelling points on a grid or drawing (usually in italics): triangle *ABC*
    - naming shapes or sets
  - **lower case**
    - representing unknown numbers (italics) *abc* represents the product of *a*, *b* and *c*
    - abbreviations for units: cm
  - **a mixTuRe**
    - some formulae such as $A = \frac{1}{2}bh$
- **Numbers (or numbers and letters)**
  Numbers with different relative sizes or in different positions can mean different things:
  - 2^3 means two cubed, $2 \times 2 \times 2$
  - $2a$ means $2 \times a$ or $a + a$
  - a^2 means *a* squared, $a \times a$
  - 6cm^2 means 6 square centimetres
  - xy^2 means $x \times y \times y$ $(xy)^2$ means $x \times y \times x \times y$
  - t_2 means the second term of sequence t_n
- **Equals sign**
  - used instead of the word 'is': $AB = 3$cm
  - used in a statement of fact: $3 + 2 = 5$
  - used in an equation: $3x + 5 = 23$
  - used to mean 'gives': $4(x - 3) = 4x - 12$
- **Negative** and **minus**
  - **negative**
    - ⁻2 (negative 2) is a number; it can stand alone
    - ⁻2 can be a position on a number line or scale e.g. temperature
    - ⁻2 can represent a movement (left or down)
  - **minus** or subtract
    - –2 (minus 2) does not stand alone
    - – is an operation as in $7 - 2 = 5$

- **Words** can have several meanings:
  - axis
    - x and y axes on a co-ordinate grid
    - axis of rotational symmetry of a solid shape
    - line of symmetry of a plane shape
  - sum
    - the result of adding two or more numbers
    - any routine calculation
  - graph
    - a line or curve on a co-ordinate grid representing a function
    - sometimes (incorrectly) to indicate a grid
    - used in the names of special diagrams:
      line graph, bar graph, scatter graph etc.
- **Zero**
  - sometimes referred to as 'nought' or 'nothing'
  - sometimes read as 'oh' (in 'phone numbers)
  - is a numeral as well as a number
  - numeral zeros on the left are not significant but we write them in numbers such as 037° (bearings), 0730 (time), 0.37 (decimals)
  - zeros in the middle are always significant
  - zeros on the right are sometimes significant but it is not always clear:
    6200 could be exact, 6204 written to the nearest 10 or 6247 written to the nearest 100
    6.20 could be exact or 6.197 written to the nearest hundredth
  - zero can mean no chance in probability
  - zero is a position on a number line half way between $^-1$ and 1
  - (0,0), the **origin**, is where the axes on a grid cross.